MW01492303

ENCOUNTERING
THE
FACE OF GOD

40 DAYS OF ENCOUNTERS

RICHIE ROOT

ROOTLEGACY
PUBLISHING

Editing: Sally Hanan of Inksnatcher.com
Book Layout: BookDesignTemplates.com
Cover Design: Richie Root

Ordering Information:
Quantity sales. Special discounts are available on quantity purchases by corporations, associations, and others. For details, contact the author at the e-mail address above.

Encountering the Face of God/Richie Root
ISBN 978-0-692-93494-4

I would like to dedicate this book to my grandparents Richard and Ruth Wiseman. They lit me on fire for the Lord when I was a little boy. Thank you so much for your love and your legacy! This is for you.

CONTENTS

FOREWORD

Everyone one day will encounter the face of God! For the followers of Jesus, that means we will see him in all his glory, sitting next to the Father, at his right hand. We will be stunned by his beauty that fills the heavens. Everything we've ever thought about Jesus will be upgraded and changed. Perfect love will wash over our souls and we will discover our eternal destiny.

Deep inside the human heart is a desire to know God intimately—not simply as one who runs the universe, but as one who knows us, understands our longings, and still loves us. It is what makes us human beings—we have an innate desire to know our Creator. The joyful discovery comes when we realize that God is waiting for us! He is watching and waiting for us to take the step of faith and expectation into his presence! How he loves to show us his face. Grace has a face, and it's smiling.

Many of us hold thoughts about God that are simply not true. The one title, the one name he wants us to use when we come before him is Father. Sadly, our human fathers have failed us. But our heavenly Father will never fail us. He dwells beyond the realm of failure, disappointment, and sadness. His presence is effervescent, giving life and strength and love to all who stand before him. To encounter God is to encounter the sweet fountain of forgiveness and mercy. It is to drink from the deepest spring of life. The face of God brings fire and passion to our souls. To find out who God truly is will leave you breathless—overcome with a longing to be close to him.

I have known Richie Root for a number of years and have found him to be a man of passionate love for Jesus. It shines through every page. He has uncovered some amazing secrets into God's heart. Born out of a quest to know God, Richie has left us a road map that will take you past the outer court into an encounter with the face of God. Each day brings you closer and closer to that encounter. Each page unveils more of God's kindness. This book will bring you into an encounter with God's goodness. I can see, after reading this excellent 40-day devotional, that all who read it will be drawn closer and closer to heaven. Richie will clearly convince you that God has left the door open and the light on, inviting you in! Answer that call and find him as the God and Father you've always wanted.

So now, you hold in your hand a book that contains keys to encountering the face of God.

Read it daily and share it with your friends. But most of all, be prepared to find the God who is more than enough for every difficulty and test you face in life. May you enjoy your journey!

Brian Simmons

The Passion Translation Project

Prologue

It's by no accident that you picked up this book. In it, I hope to take you from an encounter with God to a lifestyle of encountering him on a daily basis.

Your maker has always been right in front of you, but it takes an encounter to see him there. Adam and Eve could—they walked and talked with God in the garden every day, and then they lost it all. Since then, God has been chasing and pursuing his people, wanting to restore them to that intimate relationship he once had with them in the garden, just as he does with you. Through Jesus, you can enter that garden again, and when God reveals himself to you, you'll experience a level of intimacy that's off the charts.

The disciple John had a revelation that he was the one Jesus loved (John 13:23), and he called himself that in his writings, because Jesus probably told him he loved him. God is more eager to hang with you than you are to hang out with him because of his love for you. Like John, you can be as close to God as you want; all you need to do is spend time with God, as you need to in any good relationship. The Bible says to come near to God and he'll come near to you (James

4:8). There's no Off button or condition to that time together with him. God is a rewarder of those who seek his face.

How would you love to see God reveal himself today? How hungry are you to encounter the face of God? Some people are satisfied by Sunday services alone, but who wouldn't want to experience God in the fullest level of intimacy possible, face-to-face with him, just as Jesus did? How much of God would you like? If the decision is up to you, then what are you waiting for?

Richie Root

BEFORE YOU BEGIN

ENCOUNTER THE LOVE OF GOD

EPHESIANS 3:19

To know the love of Christ which passes knowledge;
that you may be filled with all the fullness of God.

INSIGHT

There's no one on earth or in heaven who can love you as much as God. "For God so loved the world that He gave His only begotten Son, that whoever believes in Him should not perish but have everlasting life" (John 3:16). "This is how we know what love is: Jesus Christ laid down his life for us" (1 John 3:16 NIV). His love for you was demonstrated on a simple cross.

There's nothing you can do to make him love you more. He loves you to his fullest capacity right now. You're the apple of his eye, the very one he desires to be with. When you let that sink into your heart and mind, then you know you're truly a son or daughter of God.

God is love, so true love is an actual person, not worldly love. God invites you to walk across his threshold of love and into intimacy with him. This kind of relationship surpasses knowledge and fills you up with the fullness of God. God's love was designed to fill you with the absolute fullness of God the Father, Son, and Holy Spirit.

PRAYER

He's ready to give all the fullness of himself away, so today, if you want to be filled with the fullness of God, simply receive his love toward you. If you're serious about this, read the following prayer out loud.

God, I need you. Thank you for demonstrating what real love is by laying your life down on a cross for me. Come and fill me with your love and come into my heart. I make you my lord and savior. Come and fill me with your Holy Spirit. I want to see you face-to-face! Thank you for loving me. I'm yours.

DAY 1

GOD ENCOUNTERS WORSHIPERS

2 SAMUEL 6:22

I will be even more undignified than this.

INSIGHT

King David was ready to be whatever God wanted him to be in each season of his life: shepherd boy, giant killer, worshiper, warrior, man after God's heart. God formed Adam out of clay and breathed life into him. He formed and breathed life into David, and into us too, so our lives could be an act of worship before him.

We're seeking God in our short time here on earth, and God is seeking and pursuing us. "Therefore I urge you, brothers and sisters, by the mercies of God, to present your bodies [dedicating all of yourselves, set apart] as a living sacrifice, holy and well-pleasing to God, which is your rational (logical, intelligent) act of worship." (Romans 12:1–2 AMP).

We can present our bodies to him through worship. King David stripped down to his underwear; he took off his royal robes and kingly possessions and danced before the Lord unashamed! He humbled himself, laid down his reputation, and worshiped/pleased the Lord (2 Samuel 6:14–15). As we humble ourselves and worship him, he'll reveal himself to us.

When Jesus talked to the woman at the well, he made mention that the Father was seeking worshipers. "Your worship must engage your spirit in the pursuit of truth. That's the kind of people the Father is out looking for: those who are simply and honestly themselves before him in their worship. God is sheer being itself—Spirit. Those who worship him must do it out of their very being, their spirits, their true selves, in adoration" (John 4:23–24 MSG).

If you had a chance to worship God in the most authentic expression of worship you could give, would you humble yourself and risk your reputation to please God?

PRAYER

God, I pray you would make us worshipers like David. Make us fearless when expressing our love and desire for you. Show us today how you want us to worship you. Show us your face!

DAY 2

FAITH

HEBREWS 11:6

But without faith it is impossible to please Him, for he who comes to God must believe that He is, and that He is a rewarder of those who diligently seek Him.

INSIGHT

For all the different activities that happen in life, seeking God is our greatest adventure. God loves to reward us when we seek his face. I'm beginning to realize more and more that God loves to hide himself so he can be found. An old mentor of mine in YWAM said to me once, "Don't just be busy to be busy, but be about your Father's business. Find out what God is speaking to you in this season in your life and go for it!"

But how do we find out what God is speaking? When we read the Bible or listen to the spoken word, something supernatural takes place and we begin to speak God's love language. We synchronize ourselves with his heart to prepare ourselves for an encounter. Jesus said, "Most assuredly, I say to you, the Son can do nothing of Himself, but what He sees the Father do; for whatever He does, the Son also does in like manner" (John 5:19).

When we hear him and see him, we trust him. Hearing God's word is an invitation to receive more faith. "So then faith comes by hearing, and hearing by the word of God" (Romans 10:17). We can run around playing religion all our lives, but faith in action starts out of that intimate conversation we get to have with God. After we receive faith from God, we have to find out what he wants us to do with it. Faith is the fuel to get our vehicle on the right road.

The pinnacle of life is to find the face of God and make him your home. "Now faith is the substance of things hoped for, the evidence of things not seen" (Hebrews 11:1).

PRAYER

God, I pray your words would supernaturally fuel me to encounter you on a daily basis. I pray you would create opportunities for me to hear your words. I pray for supernatural memorization and a renewed mind to hear and think like you, Jesus. Thank you that you are the author of my faith in this life!

DAY 3

DO YOU HEAR GOD'S VOICE?

JOHN 10:27

My sheep hear My voice, and I know them, and they follow Me.

INSIGHT

This is perhaps one of my favorite verses in the Bible, for the sure fact that God is speaking all the time, and we get to practice hearing his voice. God can speak to us any way he wants to. Throughout Bible times, God spoke through people, dreams, visions, nature, and angels, and he still does today.

I was told there are only three voices we can hear—God's, the devil's, or our own. We can learn what his voice sounds like by studying the character of God in Scripture. We know God is loving, righteous, compassionate, faithful, just, forgiving, and merciful. As we begin to hear what we think might be God speaking, we can see if it is his voice by looking at his character. If what we're hearing doesn't line up with God's character, then it's probably not the Lord speaking. "They will by no means follow a stranger, but will flee from him, for they do not know the voice of strangers" (John 10:1–5).

Just as we have five senses to hear, see, touch, taste, and smell, we have spiritual senses to discern good from evil. Once you've silenced the devil through Scripture and taken every thought of your own captive and submitted it to God, then there's only one voice you can hear by faith—

God's. "But solid food belongs to those who are of full age, that is, those who by reason of use have their senses exercised to discern both good and evil" (Hebrews 5:14).

God has given all humanity the ability to hear his voice. Do you hear the Lord speaking to you today? I've noticed God likes to hide things for us to find at times. At other times, it's like a real dialogue between us. Ask him to help you hear his voice.

PRAYER

God, I ask that you would open up my ears and eyes to hear and see you speaking to me today. Show me what your voice sounds like. Speak to me, God. I love you! Thank you, God, for always pursuing me and never ever leaving me! I want to feel you right now, Lord! You are my shepherd. God. Speak to me now. Let me hear your voice every day. Help me to listen to what you're sharing with me today.

DAY 4

THE KINGDOM MINDSET

MATTHEW 6:10

Your kingdom come, your will be done on earth as it is in heaven.

INSIGHT

When Jesus came to earth, he brought his hometown of heaven with him. The tangible reality of the kingdom of heaven went with him everywhere he went. Jesus came to preach the message of the kingdom and destroy the works of the devil (1 John 3:8). Wherever Jesus went, he taught about the kingdom of heaven and then people were saved, healed, and delivered. *Our mission is the same: to bring the wholeness of heaven to earth through intimacy with God.*

When we spend intimate time with God, our minds become renewed so much that we start to think like Jesus, which helps us carry out this mission of wholeness. When we live from heaven's reality, we can bring heaven to earth to prove the will of God. Colossians 3:2 says, "Set your mind on things above, not on things on the earth." Romans 12:2 says, "Do not be conformed to this world, but be transformed by the renewing of your mind, that you may prove what is that good and acceptable and perfect will of God."

God's will has always been to bring the kingdom of heaven to earth through you, to bring the *sozo* of heaven—salvation, healing, and deliverance—to everyone in your sphere of influence. That's what heaven on earth looks like—because there's no sickness, pain, poverty, depression, or disease in heaven, there shouldn't be any on earth either. These things couldn't exist near Jesus, so they shouldn't exist near you. It's time to put on the kingdom mindset and bring heaven to earth!

PRAYER

God, I pray for a kingdom mindset. I pray for a fresh perspective of what heaven looks like here on earth. Show me your reality, show me kingdom reality, show me your kingdom come on earth as it is in heaven!

DAY 5

FRIENDSHIP WITH GOD

JOHN 15:15

"No longer do I call you servants, for a servant does not know what his master is doing; but I have called you friends, for all things that I heard from My Father I have made known to you."

INSIGHT

All through history, God has been searching for friends to share his intimate secrets with. Sometimes we see our friendship with God as being the same as our friendships with our siblings and friends growing up, but friendship with God means so much more.

There are several people in the Bible who were considered friends of God. They responded to the invitation to walk with God intimately as a friend, and to lean in like the apostle John and rest their heads on Jesus's chest to listen to his heart. In Job's reminiscing about the glory days with God, he said, "Just as I was in the days of my prime, when the friendly counsel of God was over my tent; when the Almighty was yet with me, when my children were around me; when my steps were bathed with cream, and the rock poured out rivers of oil for me!" (Job 29:4–6).

A lot of people walk in relationship with God out of servanthood, but they miss out by not going deeper and developing a friendship with him. The closer we come to Jesus, the more intimate our friendship with him becomes. Today, let God do something new in your friendship with him. Give him a chance. he's the best friend you'll ever have!

PRAYER

Do you remember a time when you felt close to God? If not, say this simple prayer with me:

God, I pray for your intimate friendship and that you would share your heart with me. I want to know you more than anything! God, I want to see you face-to-face as my best friend. Would you show me the kind of friendship you're offering me? Make what you're offering easy and crystal clear.

DAY 6

WAITING UPON THE LORD

ISAIAH 40:31

But those who wait on the Lord shall renew their strength; they shall mount up with wings like eagles, they shall run and not be weary, they shall walk and not faint.

Insight

So many times in life we try and rush things or get quick results, but it's the waiting that actually strengthens us. The disciples waited for the Holy Spirit in Jerusalem, as Jesus had instructed. "Do not leave Jerusalem, but wait for the gift my Father promised, which you have heard me speak about. For John baptized with water, but in a few days you will be baptized with the Holy Spirit" (Acts 1:3–5 NIV).

Moses waited on the mountain for days before God called him up to receive the Ten Commandments (Exodus 34). If you knew God was going to show up in some kind of way, would you be willing to wait? I love how Moses put it: "If Your presence does not go with us, do not lead us up from here" (Exodus 33:14–15). When we wait upon the Lord, something supernatural happens to us. Our strength is renewed, not to mention what may be waiting for us at the end of our waiting period.

We can't be a powerful witness for God without the Holy Spirit and his power. We can only demonstrate God's love and power through the Holy Spirit. But first we must be willing to wait for the Holy Spirit. We need his presence like we need water and food to live. It's this type of mindset of waiting on and abiding in him that's going to position us for daily encounters, because He's the vine and we're his branches. Fruit can't exist without him. "Apart from me, you can do nothing" (John 15:5 NIV).

PRAYER

Holy Spirit, would you come and fill me up? I pray that you would help me wait up on you, just like my forefathers did. I need your strength. I need your power to be your witness and follower!

DAY 7

SONS AND DAUGHTERS OF GOD

(THE DNA OF GOD)

GENESIS 1:27

So God created mankind in his own image, in the image of God he created them; male and female he created them.

INSIGHT

We all carry some kind of feature we inherited from one of our parents. It may be a big or small nose, or the color of our eyes or hair. Likewise, all of us carry the very DNA of God, whether we are born again or not. We are Jesus's little brothers and sisters, and when we are born of the Spirit, we inherit everything Jesus walked in.

We grow in our identity by beholding and becoming like him. Often, we perceive him to be the way he reveals himself to us—as our healer, a good Father, our help in times of trouble. Because we've seen him display those characteristics and power, it's not a big deal for us to pray for healing, parent well, or support others when he prompts us to.

For some of us, that's not the case. A lot of us walk in this false identity of who people said we were growing up, whether through bullying or belittling. What God says about us, what he thinks about us, is what has to define our identity. How he sees us is the truth. Yes, we can have an earthly identity, like John the Baptist's or Jesus the carpenter's, but God calls us coheirs with Christ, sons and daughters of the Most High. We have an earthly identity—one other people recognize us by—and a heavenly identity, the way God sees us. It's those who live from heaven's perspective who bring their heavenly identity to earth. They know who they are.

PRAYER

God, show me who you are. Show me who I am. Show me what being a son or daughter of God, your very DNA, looks like.

DAY 8

GOD ENCOUNTERS THOSE WHO HUNGER

PSALMS 42:1–2

As the deer pants for the water brooks, so pants my soul for You, O God. My soul thirsts for God, for the living God. When shall I come and appear before God?

INSIGHT

My dad, and every other wrestling coach I had, used to say, "Go out there and get in that guy's face." I know what you're thinking, LOL. Crazy wrestling family, and yes, you're right. God loves to see his kids hunger for him. When we go chasing after him, it's only a matter of time before we get right in his face. He welcomes us to come after him and get in his face, because that's where we're created to be. At times people hide themselves from God after sinning, just like Adam and Eve did, but through Jesus, we have been restored to a relationship with God where we can walk with him face-to-face.

Right before I encountered God the first few times, I was so hungry for the living God that I was willing to do anything just to see him wink or show me a glimpse of himself. This type of posture is very standard to encountering him. God knows how hungry we are, and he also knows when we're not really interested in spending any time with him. It's my belief that God waits around for us to hang out with him, and when we do, I really believe God sings over us. "The Lord your God in your midst, the Mighty One, will save; He will rejoice over you with gladness, He will quiet you with His love,

He will rejoice over you with singing"
(Zephaniah 3:17).

God will stop at nothing to be with you on a
daily basis. his burning desire is to look in your
eyes and whisper *I love you.* You were created for
him.

PRAYER

God, would you fill me with an overwhelming
desire and hunger for you that can't be put out?
Create a discontentment inside me until I meet
you in close proximity.

DAY 9

BLESSED ARE THE PURE IN HEART

MATTHEW 5:8 NIV

Blessed are the pure in heart, for they will see God.

INSIGHT

There's a generation that's going to pursue God no matter what the cost is, just to see him face-to-face. It's God who purifies our hearts. He's just looking for a person willing to beat his chest and say *Have mercy on me, I'm a sinner.* "Who may ascend the hill of the Lord? Or who may stand in His Holy place? He who has clean hands and a pure in heart, who has not lifted up his soul to an idol, nor sworn deceitfully. He shall receive blessing from the Lord, And righteousness from the God of his salvation. This is Jacob, the generation of those who seek Him, who seek Your face" (Psalm 24:3–6).

Some of the most profound times I've had with God have been when I was adamant about meeting with him that day, because I had a lot of undealt-with junk in my heart. I knew that when I encountered God, his presence would purify me.

We can try to be clean and not sin out of our own strength. The problem with that is a religious spirit tries to sneak in and make us feel condemned if we can't do it in our own strength. The word "repent" means to change the attitude of our mind. When we step into his mind, that condemnation leaves.

How badly do you want to see God? Are you willing to be purified through the blood of the cross? It's the blood of Christ that purifies you, not your good deeds. It's the Word of God that renews your mind, and it's the Holy Spirit who empowers you!

PRAYER

God, would you purify me with your blood today? Would you do something brand new in my heart? I want to see you more than I want to hold onto my sin.

DAY 10

OPEN THE EYES OF OUR HEART

EPHESIANS 1:17–20 NIV

I keep asking that the God of our Lord Jesus Christ, the glorious Father, may give you the Spirit of wisdom and revelation, so that you may know him better. I pray that the eyes of your heart may be enlightened in order that you may know the hope to which he has called you, the riches of his glorious inheritance in his holy people, and his incomparably great power for us who believe. That power is the same as the mighty strength he exerted when he raised Christ from the dead and seated him at his right hand in the heavenly realms.

INSIGHT

The Spirit of wisdom and revelation is the Holy Spirit, our counselor and teacher. God gives the Holy Spirit to us "so that you may know him better" (v.17). I don't know about you, but I'm a little obsessed with wanting to know God in every way possible.

When we ask for the Spirit of wisdom and revelation, we're not trying to be more spiritual than anyone else, we're desiring to know him like *know* one else. It's an invitation. When we get an invitation to a wedding, we normally RSVP or decline. When we get an invitation from the Spirit who created heaven and earth, raised Jesus from the dead, and offers us everything Jesus walked in, we RSVP back that we are *all in!*

When he opens up our eyes, we can see what's going on in the heavenly realm, and we can see what God sees when we look at the people around us. The Holy Spirit reminds us of everything Jesus taught, and he directs us through our thought promptings, feelings, and every other sense. God gives us this revelation so we can encourage those around us and reveal the heart and plans of God to them.

Asking and receiving the Spirit of wisdom and revelation, in faith, was a very important *key* for

me in hearing God's voice. The Holy Spirit will
reveal heavenly revelation and give you wisdom
on how to apply it.

PRAYER

God, I pray for the Spirit of wisdom and
revelation so I can know you more each day.
Please open the eyes of my heart so I can see you.
I want to see what you see and hear what you
hear. I want you!

DAY 11

YOU WERE CREATED FOR ENCOUNTERS

1 SAMUEL 3:6–9

Then the Lord called yet again, "Samuel!" So Samuel arose and went to Eli, and said, "Here I am, for you called me." He answered, "I did not call, my son; lie down again." (Now Samuel did not yet know the Lord, nor was the word of the Lord yet revealed to him.) And the Lord called Samuel again the third time. So he arose and went to Eli, and said, "Here I am, for you did call me." Then Eli perceived that the Lord had called the boy. Therefore Eli said to Samuel, "Go, lie down; and it shall be, if He calls you, that you must say, 'Speak, Lord, for Your servant hears."

INSIGHT

My first encounter was a whisper. One early morning, when I was nineteen, I awoke to the sound of my name being whispered very loudly. *Richie,* the voice said. I got up and went to go see who had called my name, only to find my brothers were gone and my mom and dad were still sound asleep downstairs. I went back to bed and thought *I must be losing it or something.* Not until later on did I realize God was speaking to me that morning.

Perhaps you have heard your name being called out in a like manner and have wondered what it meant, or wondered how you should've responded to God speaking to you. Sometimes God's voice sounds like your own voice in your mind, and you think it's just one of your own thoughts. Think again. There is a difference between hearing God speak inside your mind or heart and audibly hearing him. A lot of times you'll hear God's voice internally.

For some of us, we've been listening to God's voice our whole lives and never known it. Even our gut feelings about things might be God watching out for us and trying to direct us. So many times we try and write off these thoughts in our heads, and we just assume it's us, but the

Holy Spirit often teaches, guides, comforts, and supports us through our thoughts to prepare us for the things God is going to do. Sometimes our gut feeling is just the devil trying to make us fearful of something, which is why it's so important to learn how to recognize God's voice.

God has the ability to tap into your brain right now and know everything. The Bible even says his thoughts toward you outnumber the grains of sands of the sea (Psalm 139:17–18). God knit you in your mother's womb, *and you were created to encounter him.* That's why you're here on planet earth.

PRAYER

God, thank you that you know every thought I have. Help me to recognize which thoughts are mine and which are yours, so I can know your voice when you speak.

DAY 12

ENCOUNTER THE FACE OF THE BROKEN

MATTHEW 25:40 NIV

"Whatever you did for one of the least of these brothers and sisters of mine, you did for me."

INSIGHT

As we pursue the face of God, we have to remember we're living in a broken world, and we have been asked by God to bring heaven to earth.

God talked about Abel's spilled blood crying out to him for justice (Genesis 4:10). Nothing goes unseen or unheard by God. The Bible talks about how he will wipe away every tear that falls on the ground, but he expects us to be like Jesus on earth and bring heaven to everyone. "For I was hungry and you gave me something to eat, I was thirsty and you gave me something to drink, I was a stranger and you invited me in, I needed clothes and you clothed me, I was sick and you looked after me, I was in prison and you came to visit me" (Matthew 25:35–36 NIV).

Millions of people are currently enslaved worldwide. Men, women, and children are sold into forced labor or prostitution. My wife and I have partnered with organizations that work toward the abolition of child trafficking through prevention, rescue missions, and aftercare. Just as God called Moses to free the slaves out of Egypt, he's called the church to free those who are in spiritual chains, as well as those who are in physical chains in the world of human trafficking.

This is where we get to be heroes! God invites us into the plan of his ministry, his mission, his restoration of all things. You and I get to restore the world, with him leading the charge! Not to mention all the heavenly angels right by your side. Make no mistake about it, we're living in an unseen battle, and we have to get in the game because following God is a full-contact sport!

PRAYER

God, I pray that you would break my heart for the things that break yours! Give me insight and understanding of how personally it affects you when the weak cry out for help. Today, God, make me a hero with you. Let me encounter you in defending the weak. Show me my place in your mighty army!

DAY 13

ENCOUNTER GOD THROUGH FRIENDS

MARK 2:3–5 NIV

Some men came, bringing to him a paralyzed man, carried by four of them. Since they could not get him to Jesus because of the crowd, they made an opening in the roof above Jesus by digging through it and then lowered the mat the man was lying on. When Jesus saw their faith, he said to the paralyzed man, "Son, your sins are forgiven."

INSIGHT

God loves to heal his kids more than we can understand, and he'll use any means necessary. One of his favorite ways is through community. We need one another to thrive in life. We're as strong as the people we surround ourselves with. Throughout history, we've seen incredible accomplishments through numbers of people working together in unity. All throughout the Bible, we see this pattern of believers working together as friends, like Moses and Joshua, David and Jonathan, Paul and Barnabas. Jesus's presence shows up powerfully in community: "For where two or three are gathered together in My name, I am there in the midst of them" (Matthew 18:20).

God is attracted to groups of people coming together in his name! There have been times in my life when I wasn't connecting with God, for whatever reason, but I had a group of guys around me to encourage and pick me up. God uses friends to encourage, confront, keep us accountable, listen, pray, and speak truth. The Bible says we are the body of Christ, and we need one another to function "so that the body of Christ may be built up until we all reach unity in the faith and in the knowledge of the Son of God and become mature" (Ephesians 4:12–13).

Jesus was moved when he saw the faith of the paralyzed man's friends, and their willingness to rip off the roof of a house just to lower their friend to meet him. Do you have friends like this? If not, imagine filling your life with men and women who would have your back through every valley and mountaintop.

PRAYER

God, I pray that you would surround me with mighty men and women with stronger faith than mine. Help me to be transparent with, and open to being accountable to, someone a little more mature than me. Remove any pride that prevents me from wanting to thrive and grow in the community you've given me.

DAY 14

OBEDIENCE = SEEING THE FACE OF GOD

DEUTERONOMY 28:2

And all these blessings shall come upon you and overtake you, because you obey the voice of the Lord your God.

INSIGHT

I've seen God show up time and time again in my life because I sensed him asking me to do something and I followed through with it. *When we're obedient to whatever God asks us to do, there's a blessing waiting on the other side.*

When I was a kid, I heard promises from my parents like: If you eat all your dinner, you'll get a dessert. Well, the blessings of God are like dessert. God wants to give you good things every day of your life, but *first* he wants to hang out with you and share his heart and mind with you, because that's what friends do. I don't know about you, but I'd rather have hang time with God face-to-face than just see his hand give me another blessing.

For the longest time, we've gotten the journey mixed up with the summit. Yes, we get to stand in awe once we get to the top and enjoy the blessings of the view, but it's the intimate journey with God along the way—of communing with him and learning his heart's mission for our lives—that helps us ultimately get to know him.

You get to know him by obeying his personalized promptings through the ways he speaks to you. He has a love language of his heart designed only for you. There's no one else who can fill that listening role but you. Obedience to God is what defines a successful life, not all your riches, wealth, and achievements.

PRAYER

Today I pray, God, that you would really help me with obedience, even when it's hard. Help me to listen, obey, and follow through with your heart's mission for my life.

DAY 15

HEAVEN AND EARTH'S CURRENCY

MATTHEW 6:21

Where your treasure is, there your heart will be also.

INSIGHT

Everything that was given to humanity was given for the purpose of building heaven on earth. "We make a living by what we get, we make a life by what we give away" (Winston Churchill). Like anything, what's used for good can be used for bad. If we pour money into the wrong investments, we'll have no returns, but if we invest in building heaven on earth, we're going to see limitless returns.

Money is kind of like a heart gauge. God doesn't need our money, but he uses it to unlock heaven from our hearts. When we surrender things that are dear to us, like money, God notices. Everything already belongs to God, according the Bible, so God expects us to spend the simple Monopoly© money he's given us in a way that demonstrates where our heart really is.

As there are laws that govern this world's economy, there are laws that govern heaven's economy. The kingdom is inside you (Luke 17:21), ready to invest. God allows us to partner with him on earth by sowing or investing in the best kingdom stocks (areas God tells us to invest in) with the best returns. The more kingdom stocks of love we have, the more we're going to encounter God, because his plans to encounter all humanity are really important.

As money is the currency of earth, love is the currency of heaven. That's why money and the love in our hearts mirror each other from two different worlds. Our money is no good in heaven, but the expansion of love in our hearts on earth is the expansion of the kingdom. If we use heaven's currency on earth, we begin to expand and build the kingdom.

There are keys of money and love that unlock heaven in people's lives very easily, and then there are keys that have to be strategically placed in the right doors to open. When heaven shows up, guess who's sitting on that throne waiting to encounter you? Invest in the kingdom if you want to see who sits on the throne!

PRAYER

God, thank you that you own everything and you allow me access to it. Would you expand your love and kingdom in my heart? Show me which kingdom stocks you want me to invest in, Lord. I want to see your kingdom in a powerful way, and see you sitting on your throne, more than anything!

DAY 16

ENCOUNTER HIS BEAUTY

PSALM 27:4 NIV

One thing I ask from the Lord, this only do I seek: that I may dwell in the house of the Lord all the days of my life, to gaze on the beauty of the Lord and to seek him in his temple.

INSIGHT

All it takes is one look to forever be changed. Throughout history, the men, women, and children who encountered God were forever addicted to his presence and beauty after gazing upon him. There's definitely an awe-filled, jaw-dropping moment when you first encounter God. his reality all of a sudden becomes yours! Your faith skyrockets, and your encounter becomes a great faith-building memory you return to in coming days.

When you abandon everything else to encounter him, you discover his face, touch, smell, and voice, and you taste that the Lord is good! "For David says in regard to Him, I saw the Lord constantly before me, for He is at my right hand that I may not be shaken or overthrown or cast down [from my secure and happy state]" (Acts 2:25 AMPC).

I believe God encounters us in stages. First, he takes us through introductions, and then to big and small encounters. Then I believe God invites us into a lifestyle of encountering him on a daily basis. This is sometimes hard for people who aren't encountering God to understand. It's easy to get caught up in the crossfire of being judged by those who don't understand the reality you've been invited to live in.

This is where you ask God for wisdom from above, so you can respond to them wisely and build community through it. "But the wisdom that is from above is first pure, then peaceable, gentle, willing to yield, full of mercy and good fruits, without partiality and without hypocrisy" (James 3:17). "Real wisdom, God's wisdom, begins with a holy life and is characterized by getting along with others. It is gentle and reasonable, overflowing with mercy and blessings, not hot one day and cold the next, not two-faced. You can develop a healthy, robust community that lives right with God and enjoy its results only if you do the hard work of getting along with each other, treating each other with dignity and honor" (James 3:17–18 MSG).

PRAYER

God, I long to see your beauty! One thing I ask and this is what I seek, that I may gaze upon your beauty and look you in the eyes! I love you, and I can't wait to see you!

DAY 17

INVITATION FOR AN ENCOUNTER

JEREMIAH 33:3 NIV

"Call to me and I will answer you and tell you great and unsearchable things you do not know."

INSIGHT

Time after time, God invites us into an encounter with him. There's truly nothing like it when he initiates an intimate meeting with us. "After this I looked, and there before me was a door standing open in heaven. And the voice I had first heard speaking to me like a trumpet said, "'Come up here, and I will show you what must take place after this'" (Revelation 4:1 NIV). It's one thing to pursue God, it's another to be chased down by him.

We can't out love God, no matter how hard we try. Just like his thoughts toward us never end, so his love and affections never end. So many times in life, I find myself trying to work for God's love, when there's nothing I can do but just receive it as his child.

There's so much God wants to share with us every day, but he knows we can only handle so much. He's spoken to his kids billions and billions of times, in both simple to complex, and mysterious to straightforward ways. Imagine being chased by the most intense lion on earth your whole life. Eventually that four-hundred-pound lion is going to get you. God will have his way.

He'll make it known to all creation that he is pursuing his kids. He will stop at nothing until he finds you and picks you up and holds you. You've always been his. It's time to encounter him!

PRAYER

God, I want to encounter you in such a powerful way that it brands me for life. Bring me close and let me look at you face-to-face, as a child looks into his Father's eyes. Come Lion of Judah! Come and catch me!

DAY 18

ENCOUNTER THE JOY OF THE LORD

PSALM 16: 11

You will show me the path of life; in Your presence is fullness of joy; at Your right hand are pleasures forevermore.

INSIGHT

Each encounter has a different purpose. God will reveal some of his many characteristics when we come into close proximity with him, depending on what we need in each encounter. He may encounter us to invite us on an exploit, or to love on us with no assignment.

One of the normal atmospheres God manifests is pure joy. In his presence is truly the fullness of joy and peace. I remember going through some very hard seasons of my life, and God offered me joy in the midst of the huge storms. "Do not sorrow, for the joy of the Lord is your strength" (Nehemiah 8:10). I began to realize navigating through life outside his presence was a very hard atmosphere to live in. Jesus said, "In this world you will have trouble. But take heart! I have overcome the world" (John 16:33). It's so much easier to face a storm with his presence navigating you vs. wandering without direction. Having God's peace means sleeping like Jesus did in the boat while in the midst of the storm.

Jesus walked in the joy of Lord, in that he knew he was the Father's joy. The joy of the Lord is a tangible, manifest presence that's transferable, but the joy of Lord is also a deep revelation and understanding that *you bring the Lord joy!* You are

Papa God's joy! You're his delight! You make him *happy!* There's something so freeing and empowering when you know you bring joy to God the Father. Walking in this mindset and atmosphere is your strength. When Christians start living with this mindset while the devil's trying to tear them down, they'll be unstoppable.

PRAYER

God, I pray for the joy of Lord! Come and fill me, Holy Spirit, with the fruit of joy. I need your joy. Give me the revelation that I am Papa's joy.

DAY 19

Jesus Is God

John 14::8–10

Philip said to Him, "Lord, show us the Father, and it is sufficient for us." Jesus said to him, "Have I been with you so long, and yet you have not known Me, Philip? He who has seen Me has seen the Father; so how can you say, 'Show us the Father?' Do you not believe that I am in the Father, and the Father in Me?"

INSIGHT

Jesus is the son of God, according to Scripture, but he's also God, and fully human as well. If you have been looking for the face of God, Jesus said, "Anyone who has seen me has seen the Father" (v.9). Every book of the Bible points to Jesus Christ as the final destination and meaning of life. "He is the image of the invisible God, the firstborn over all creation. For by Him all things were created that are in heaven and that are on earth, visible and invisible, whether thrones or dominions or principalities or powers. All things were created through Him and for Him. And He is before all things, and in Him all things consist" (Colossians 1:15–18).

If you've been seeking God's face, there's no chance you accidentally picked up this book. If you didn't know Jesus was God, let me tell you the greatest information you'll ever read: "Jesus said to him, 'I am the way, the truth, and the life. No one comes to the Father except through Me'" (John 14:6). This revelation helps us realize what kind of sacrifice God really demonstrated for us on the cross. If Jesus was fully human and fully God, he limited his being to suffer on our behalf. God actually felt the whips and nails driven into his body so we could encounter him through relationship.

If this whole time you've longed to encounter the face of God, you could have simply opened the red letter edition Bible and read anything in red font and heard his voice. Sometimes we make it so complicated when he just wants to encourage us to come to him with simple steps and childlike faith. The big jaw-dropping encounters are part of encountering him, but sometimes we can miss him right in front of our faces because we're looking for him in something else. Enjoy the moments and seasons God has you in, because he's designed them all for you.

PRAYER

Lord, I can see who you are by reading your words and by studying your character of love. Help me to never miss an opportunity to see your face. I want to see you in the Bible, in the people around me, in your sacrifice.

DAY 20

YOU HAVE TO DIE BEFORE YOU CAN SEE HIM

EXODUS 33:19–23

Then He said, "I will make all My goodness pass before you, and I will proclaim the name of the LORD before you. I will be gracious to whom I will be gracious, and I will have compassion on whom I will have compassion." But He said, "You cannot see My face; for no man shall see Me, and live." And the LORD said, "Here is a place by Me, and you shall stand on the rock. So it shall be, while My glory passes by, that I will put you in the cleft of the rock, and will cover you with My hand while I pass by. Then I will take away My hand, and you shall see My back; but My face shall not be seen."

INSIGHT

The greatest journey you can take in this life is the one in which you encounter the face of the living God. This journey, though, will cost you everything you have. In every area of your life, you will have to journey through the desert for a while to be tested like Jesus — to see if you're willing to settle for less than God's face. You'll pass a lot of the tests but will fail some too. You'll come up against impossible tests that require his power to even stay the path, but with him you'll make it through to the place where abiding in him is your only way to live life.

"I've been crucified with Christ and I no longer live, but Christ lives in me" (Galatians 2:20) will become a reality. Christ will be formed in you, and his thoughts will run through your mind all day and night because you'll be carrying the mind of Christ. You will be transformed from glory to glory into his image. After all, you were made in it. Then you will begin to encounter him on a daily basis, communing and walking with him like Jesus did while on earth. It'll be similar to Adam's walks with God in the garden, only better.

PRAYER

God, I pray for your grace to walk in this lifestyle of continually encountering you on a daily basis. I accept your invitation to walk with you closely like this. Remove any fear or religious spirit that would stop me from running all the way to your throne. Lord, you tell me to come boldly to your throne! Thank you, God. Let's do this!

DAY 21

EVERY ENCOUNTER HAS A PURPOSE

MARK 5:30 MSG

At the same moment, Jesus felt energy discharging from him. He turned around to the crowd and asked, "Who touched my robe?"

INSIGHT

Since the first time I felt the manifest presence of God, I became addicted and wanted to spend way more time with God, all because I'd encountered him. I was in a dorm room on a YWAM base in Montana. As I was waiting on the Lord and playing my guitar softly, I felt some kind of supernatural hand touching my upper back. Immediately, I turned around in shock. There was no one there. Again I began to play my guitar, and sure enough, I felt a hand on fire touching my back. I continued playing and started crying in awe of what was happening to me. Was I going crazy or making this up in my head?

From that point on, when I sat down with my guitar to worship the Lord, I did it with the purpose of intimately engaging God. God wasn't just interested in hearing me sing, he wanted to love on me and minister to the deepest places of my heart. *His purpose for us was intimacy with him, and so I made my purpose with him intimacy.*

When we come close to God and feel him put his arm around us, there's nothing we won't do. We all have our own unique way of hearing from God. God knows how we need to be loved today and every day.

Just as everyone has a primary love language, we have a primary way to hear from God — through our spiritual senses, as I shared in the previous chapter. For some of us, this is exactly how we discern and hear from God for others. I know a man who feels the Lord touch the fingers on his left hand when God is calling someone into a season of teaching, pastoring, evangelizing, prophesying, or fathering. Jesus felt power leave his body when the woman touched his robe (Mark 25:25–32). Every encounter is custom designed for God's sons and daughters. Every encounter has a purpose.

PRAYER

God, I want to feel your presence the way Jesus felt you. Would you touch me, Holy Spirit, and break through anything that resists your manifest presence? I want to feel your presence so badly. Break through my flesh, break through my lack of faith and my doubts. Come and rest upon me, Holy Spirit. I pray for intimate fellowship with you. Thank you for your presence!

DAY 22

ENCOUNTER GOD IN DREAMS

GENESIS 28:16–17

"Surely the Lord is in this place, and I did not know it." And he was afraid and said, "How awesome is this place! This is none other than the house of God, and this is the gate of heaven!

INSIGHT

God loves to speak to us in dreams. Think about it: the only time we intentionally rest is when we're asleep at night. The Bible is full of stories of God speaking through people in their dreams to warn them or direct them in the path they should go. There are so many biblical characters who received dreams from the Lord for direction for their lives. The sad thing is the church has written off dreams for so many years because the New Agers came out with their dream interpretation resources.

God gave Joseph the ability to interpret dreams to influence Pharaoh. God also gave Daniel the same gifting to influence Nebuchadnezzar, king of Babylon. My favorite dream of all time is when Jacob went to the place he ended up naming Bethel and dreamed of angels ascending and descending on a ladder: "Then he dreamed, and behold, a ladder was set up on the earth, and its top reached to heaven; and there the angels of God were ascending and descending on it. And behold, the Lord stood above it and said: . . . Behold, I am with you and will keep you wherever you go, and will bring you back to this land; for I will not leave you until

I have done what I have spoken to you" (Genesis 28:10–16).

I get so much direction for my life through God speaking to me at night.

PRAYER

God, I pray for increased dreams in the night. I pray you would speak to me through dreams and visions, and give me direction for my life and encouragement for others. I ask for the gift of interpretation so I may know what my dreams are about. Thank you in advance, God.

DAY 23

ENCOUNTERING HIS FACE THROUGH RECONCILIATION, PENIEL (THE FACE OF GOD)

GENESIS 32: 22–30

That night Jacob . . . was left alone, and a man wrestled with him till daybreak. When the man saw that he could not overpower him, he touched the socket of Jacob's hip so that his hip was wrenched as he wrestled with the man. Then the man said, . . . "Your name will no longer be Jacob, but Israel, because you have struggled with God and with humans and have overcome." . . . Then he blessed him there. So Jacob called the place Peniel, saying, "It is because I saw God face-to-face, and yet my life was spared."

INSIGHT

If you want to see the face of God, you have to be willing to wrestle (grapple, fight for, contend) him, no matter what the outcome may be. As I said on Day 8, I grew up in a big-time wrestling family. My mom would get down on the carpet with us and demonstrate wrestling moves because my dad was too big for my brothers and me; but every once in a while, us kids would grab a hold of our dad and attempt to wrestle him. My dad used to say to us boys, "Win, lose, or draw, I love ya." It's the same idea with God. He wants us to come wrestle with him because he wants to show us his face.

My brothers and I used to help train a former UFC Champion named Rich Franklin, who didn't grow up wrestling. Instead he was trained in karate, jiu-jitsu, boxing, and other skills. He was one tough competitor, for the sure fact he fought against the greatest UFC fighters of his day. Like him, any lack of skills you think you have shouldn't hold you back from achieving your goals in life. If you're going to go after the face of God, you might need to turn up the intensity. There's a real blessing in wrestling with God. He doesn't care whether you win, lose, or draw. he just loves you! Quit worrying about *what* you're lacking and realize *who* you have.

Jacob told the angel he would not let him go unless he blessed him. That's the kind of determination and intensity you must go after God with. "'No, please!' said Jacob. 'If I have found favor in your eyes, accept this gift from me. *For to see your face is like seeing the face of God*, now that you have received me favorably. Please accept the present that was brought to you, for God has been gracious to me and I have all I need.' And because Jacob insisted, Esau accepted it" (Genesis 33:10–11 NIV, emphasis mine). When Jacob and Esau made up from a long, knockdown, drag out fight, Jacob compared the wrestling and reconciliation to his experience the night before, when he was wrestling God, seeing him face-to-face, and receiving a blessing because of his persistence.

God has given us the ministry of reconciliation to reconcile the world back to him. There are billions and billions of people longing to see the face of God, and if we are willing to go after his call, we can lead them to that pursuit and blessing of an encounter of reconciliation with God. Our highest achievements in life don't even come close to looking God in the eyes and hearing him say well done, good and faithful servant. God wants us to introduce him to the rest of world. When we operate in the ministry of reconciliation, we introduce the rest of the world to their greatest longing—the face of Jesus.

PRAYER

God, I pray you would show me right now everyone you want me to introduce to you. I pray those people would encounter you tonight in their dreams, or through some supernatural breakthrough.

DAY 24

PAUL ENCOUNTERED GOD

PSALM 34:5 NIV

Those who look to him are radiant.

INSIGHT

When Saul (Paul) encountered Jesus on the road to Damascus, he had a radical conversion. He went from killing Christians to leading them and became the apostle Paul. "As he journeyed he came near Damascus, and suddenly a light shone around him from heaven. Then he fell to the ground, and heard a voice saying to him, Saul, Saul, why are you persecuting Me? And he said, 'Who are You, Lord?' The Lord said, 'I am Jesus, whom you are persecuting.' . . . So he, trembling and astonished, said, 'Lord what do You want me to do?' Then the Lord said to him 'Arise and go into the city, and you will be told what you must do'" (Acts 9:3–6).

Paul was literally blinded by the heavenly light and couldn't see until Ananias prayed for him. So God took the most dangerous man to the Christian faith and recruited him to help lead the church!

Imagine the most dangerous people on earth encountering Jesus. Now try imagining every human being on earth encountering him right now and forever being changed. I love how Bill Johnson puts it: "We owe the world an encounter with God."

You were created to always live in his presence and his gaze. How do you share what you've experienced? People are looking for love, and they need a real encounter with the face of love. We've all been given our own sphere of influence in life, and we get to share an encounter with God in it.

PRAYER

God, I pray for a radical encounter with you like the one Paul experienced on the road to Damascus. I pray every human being on planet earth could encounter you in life-changing ways. Help me to fix my eyes on you, God, that I may be radiant.

DAY 25

ISAIAH ENCOUNTERS GOD

ISAIAH 6:1–5 NIV

I saw the Lord, high and exalted, seated on a throne; and the train of his robe filled the temple. Above him were seraphim, each with six wings: With two wings they covered their faces, with two they covered their feet, and with two they were flying. And they were calling to one another: 'Holy, holy, holy is the Lord Almighty; the whole earth is full of his glory.' At the sound of their voices the doorposts and thresholds shook and the temple was filled with smoke. 'Woe to me!' I cried. 'I am ruined! For I am a man of unclean lips, and I live among a people of unclean lips, and my eyes have seen the King, the Lord Almighty.'

INSIGHT

Talk about an encounter! Close your eyes and try and imagine the Lord standing on the throne with his arms wide open, and he's looking straight at you with a smile. If that's hard to do, then maybe ask God to show you his face. Say, Lord, I want to see you more than anything, and I don't care if it kills me. I have to see you face-to-face! Show me what Isaiah saw, show me your face, Lord.

I still remember being in awe when God showed up in my life. I was blown away. *He's really real* I said to myself after I felt him for the first time. I was in shock, and my emotions didn't know what to do. And then of course, because I was very young in my walk with God, I blurted my story out to everyone, and they just stared at me like I was crazy. Jesus talked about not throwing your pearls to pigs. When God shows you something that unique and surreal in your life, it's normally for you, or for you to encourage someone with. There are plenty of times I don't share an encounter and just ponder or pray through it. Sometimes God wants you to be left in awe and not figure it out. He's good at doing that actually. I'm sure Isaiah had a hard time sharing his encounter.

Remember, God chose to encounter you for a reason. He's always intentional about everything he does. I'm convinced that sometimes God allows you to experience the level of intensity of an encounter for the level of intensity of a calling. It's the encounter that prepares you for any assignment. Paul, Isaiah, Moses—none of them had an easy assignment from God, but they all were launched into their callings after an encounter.

PRAYER

God, I pray for an encounter so extravagant that it launches me into the calling you have for me in life.

DAY 26

ELIJAH ENCOUNTERED GOD

1 KINGS 19:11–13 NIV

The Lord said, "Go out and stand on the mountain in the presence of the Lord, for the Lord is about to pass by." Then a great and powerful wind tore the mountains apart and shattered the rocks before the Lord, but the Lord was not in the wind. After the wind there was an earthquake, but the Lord was not in the earthquake. After the earthquake came a fire, but the Lord was not in the fire. And after the fire came a gentle whisper. When Elijah heard it, he pulled his cloak over his face and went out and stood at the mouth of the cave. Then a voice said to him, "What are you doing here, Elijah?"

INSIGHT

I'll be honest, every time I read this chapter, I'm speechless. Try to imagine the mountains being torn down right in front of you, followed by an earthquake, fire, and, not to mention, God whispering right after that. Speechless! Talk about having a story to brag to your friends about. Notice, Elijah didn't pull his hood over his head until he heard God whisper his name.

When I read stories like this, I realize more and more that God is capable of anything, *and he only showed Elijah a portion of his power*! I stand in awe and just begin to dream with God. Matthew 19:26 says "with God all things are possible." Now apply this to your day. What impossibilities are you facing today? Does someone dear to you need some kind of healing and encouragement? Know that God is bigger and greater than it all. "Surely the arm of the Lord is not too short to save, nor his ear too dull to hear" (Isaiah 59:1).

PRAYER

I want you to begin to do things a little differently today. I want you to start praying like your prayers *do* get heard by God and he *is* going to move on your behalf, because you're a son or daughter of his. I want you to imagine that everything you're praying for is going to come to pass and start thanking him as though it's already happened.

Example: Thank you, God, for healing my friend Tina who had cancer. Thank you, God, for getting my friend a job. Thank you, God, for introducing yourself to my friend Rob who didn't know you. Thank you, God, for my friend being touched by your power and now he doesn't struggle with pain anymore. Thank you that I can talk to you like this, God, because you're my dad and you care about me. I love you!

DAY 27

ENCOUNTER HIS EYES

REVELATION 19:12–13,15–16 NIV

His eyes are like blazing fire, and on his head are many crowns. He has a name written on him that no one knows but he himself. He is dressed in a robe dipped in blood, and his name is the Word of God. . . . Coming out of his mouth is a sharp sword with which to strike down the nations. . . . He treads the winepress of the fury of the wrath of God Almighty. On his robe and on his thigh he has this name written: king of kings and lord of lords.

INSIGHT

I don't know what comes to your mind when you read that, but I'll admit, the fear of the Lord kicks in gear when I read it. His eyes are flames of fire that gaze into your whole being. Once you lock eyes with him like that, it's like missile lock-on and you can't shake him off. His love at one glance is so penetrating that you know you're in the presence of eternal love that purifies by fire.

The return of Christ is by far the most powerful event that will ever take place on earth in human history. I love the contrast between Jesus coming to earth as the Lamb of God two thousand years ago and his return to earth as the Lion of Judah in the coming days. The Lord loves to reveal himself differently at times. Sometimes it's based on the season he has us in, and at other times it's just how he wants to reveal himself because he's God.

Sometimes when you focus and direct your attention and faith on certain characteristics in God, he reveals that trait you're looking for. He might show himself to you as a warrior, a shepherd, or a gardener. He wants you to be curious about the many ways you can encounter his face.

PRAYER

Before, no one could see your face and live. God, I
want to see your eyes from this day forward.
God, I want to see your burning desire for me.
Show me your eyes and everything you see. Let
your perfect love drive out all fear and let me
melt into you, God.

DAY 28

MOSES ENCOUNTERED I AM

EXODUS 3:15–15 NIV

God said to Moses, "I am who I am. This is what you are to say to the Israelites: 'I am has sent me to you.'" God also said to Moses, "Say to the Israelites, 'The Lord, the God of your fathers—the God of Abraham, the God of Isaac and the God of Jacob—has sent me to you.' This is my name forever, the name you shall call me from generation to generation."

INSIGHT

Moses was driven from his palatial home and princely life in Egypt to the desert, where he shepherded sheep for forty years. Near the end of that time in the desert, he encountered God through a burning bush—God appeared before him as a consuming fire. As I've said in other chapters, God reveals himself a lot of times in the way we perceive him, but in this case, God revealed himself the way he wanted Moses to lead, as a man on fire. Moses went from being a prince of Egypt to a shepherd to a man on fire for God, and one of the most powerful figures in the ancient world.

Many of us are right on the very edge of encountering God for the first time in our lives, after many years of waiting. Prepare and position your heart for his presence, because it's your time to stand in front of the consuming fire of his love. His eyes are on you and he wants you to feel the overwhelming, passionate love he has for you! This kind of encounter was designed to light you on fire as a man or woman of God. Behold and become the flame! Behold and become like Jesus, the great I AM.

Jesus said: I AM the bread of life; living water; the good shepherd; the light of the world; the gate; God's Son; the resurrection; the way, the truth, and life; in the Father; the true vine; the first and the last; the living one; coming soon. He has so many other characteristics, and you can find them all in the Bible. Jesus is the great I AM looking for those who willing to encounter and carry his fire.

PRAYER

God, I pray you would reveal to me, in the Bible and throughout this life, that you are the great I AM of everything! I want to encounter you, God, just like Moses did.

DAY 29

ENCOUNTER GOD THROUGH NATURE

EXODUS 3:4

So when the LORD saw that he turned aside to look, God called to him from the midst of the bush and said, "Moses, Moses!" And he said, "Here I am."

INSIGHT

Some of the most amazing times I've spent with God have been in gatherings where everyone was chasing after God's face, and the whole room was charged with the presence of God. At other times I've been in the woods, walking on the trails with the Lord, and felt amazing peace and joy. One time I was in Papua, New Guinea, working with a tribe through Wycliff Bible Translators. The last night I was in the jungle, one of the tribal men asked me to dance with the tribe. Our helicopter was coming the next morning, so I thought, *What the heck.* They painted my face with their tribal colors and dressed me up like a warrior and gave me a drum. We danced around a fire and worshiped the Lord. I danced nonstop from eleven o'clock that night 'til the helicopter picked us up the next morning at eight. It was one of those times when I connected with God through nature in a very deep way.

Sometimes God calls us back to the jungle or the garden because he wants all our attention. I'll be completely honest with you and say: If this had been in my neighborhood backyard, I may have struggled to do this, unless God had really wanted me to.

There are times in life when we need to get away from our phones and our perfectly safe neighborhoods and experience God in the wild. I would love to go rent a cabin in the woods with my family for a month, with no cellphones and no Internet. Yes, the world would still function without me. As matter of fact, we're missing out on another world God offers us. Some of us need to go camping and spend some time with God in the wild, and just maybe dance around a fire like King David.

PRAYER

God, I pray I could encounter you in the wild and through nature. Show me your very fingerprints all over the earth, and how you long for me to spend real quality time with you, with no distractions from the rest of the world.

DAY 30

ENCOUNTER THE GOD WHO DELIVERS

MARK 1:34

Then He healed many who were sick with various diseases, and cast out many demons; and He did not allow the demons to speak, because they knew Him.

INSIGHT

A lot of people like to change the subject when the topic of deliverance is brought up out of a lack of understanding or fear. As I shared in one of the previous chapters, the Greek word *sozo* means saved, healed, or delivered. When the Holy Spirit opens up the gates of the kingdom of God—that's inside us all—the atmosphere of heaven comes and overwhelms the darkness.

People were healed and delivered instantly around Jesus. "But if I cast out demons by the Spirit of God, surely the kingdom of God has come upon you" (Matthew 12:28). When the demons encountered Jesus, they all freaked out and started panicking.

Walking free from bondage is part of our legal rights as sons and daughters of God. "He has delivered us from the power of darkness and conveyed us into the kingdom of the Son of His love, in whom we have redemption through His blood, the forgiveness of sins" (Colossians 1:13–14). Demons will try and get you to come into agreement with them on any lie. When the devil tempted Jesus, he used Scripture and tried to get Jesus to agree with him in his twisting of it, which was still a lie. Once you come into agreement with lies, you empower them. That's really all demons have as a power source. A lot of times, breaking free from bondage means coming out of agreement with lies and agreeing with the truth. Jesus is the truth. He said, "The enemy comes to kill steal and destroy, but I have come to give you life to the fullest" (John 10:10).

PRAYER

God, I pray you would give me life to the fullest and that I wouldn't be fearful, but aware of the enemy's lies. I pray for your perfect love to drive out all fear and darkness. I plead the blood of Jesus over me right now and declare to every unclean spirit, *Leave me now in Jesus's name.* Come and fill me up, Holy Spirit. I need you so much! I want to know you more than anything. Thank you, God, for your victory.

DAY 31

ENCOUNTER ANGELS

HEBREWS 1:14

Are they not all ministering spirits sent forth to minister for those who will inherit salvation?

INSIGHT

God is constantly at work restoring his family back to himself with all of heaven at his side, which is why God intended for angels to be as close to you as possible. Wherever you go, angels are watching out for you. They are fellow servants with you, and God invites you to partner with him and all heaven.

I've had some awesome experiences with angels in the past. After encountering them, it was very clear why God allowed me to be aware of their presence. Sometimes they show up as fire when I pray for people. That's why people sometimes feel fire when someone is praying for them. I like to think of it as angels doing surgery on someone. "And of the angels He says: 'Who makes His angels spirits and His ministers a flame of fire'" Hebrews 1:7). While I was writing this book, I encountered some angels in a brand-new way—I saw four angels descending and ascending from heaven, blowing horns at me. It really got my attention, to say the least.

Angels are closer to humans than we realize! They show up in so many ways that it's hard sometimes to know if we've entertained an angel or a regular person. At other times, they're disguised as people in our dreams and in real life.

"Do not forget to entertain strangers, for by so doing some have unwittingly entertained angels" (Hebrews 13:2).

Some people, such as kids and the pure in heart, can literally see angels. The medical field would definitely question this, but God loves their faith because he's the author it. Angels show up in the medical field and defy the secular mindset all the time. I believe hospitals will eventually be emptied as God continues to encounter the medical field.

Some of you are actually going to encounter angels as you're reading this book and are going to be completely freaked out, haha. Don't be afraid of them. When angels show up, it's because there's some kind of worship going on, or God has a very important message to share, or they're protecting you, or God wants to minister to someone. Think of them as your personal bodyguards. They may show up in a burst of light and disappear like small orbs, or they may show in dreams. Keep these encounters to yourself and don't brag to your friends about them, because you'll only sound crazy. When they show up, impossibilities bow to the name of Jesus.

PRAYER

God, I pray you would help me to be more aware of your angels so I can partner with you and heaven.

DAY 32

SEEKING THE KINGDOM—GOD'S REALITY

MATTHEW 6:33

Seek first the kingdom of God and His righteousness, and all these things shall be added unto you.

INSIGHT

So many times in life, we say something out of habit because we've heard it somewhere else, and we don't really know what it even means. We haven't done any study on the subject or verse. For instance, we can repeat how Jesus said it's useless to worry about what we'll wear or eat, but to focus on seeking his kingdom first, but we need to ask *How do we seek heaven?*

Look at another story of when Jesus encouraged his disciples to pray a certain way: "Your kingdom come. Your will be done on earth as it is in heaven" (Matthew 6:10). Jesus was a citizen of heaven, and his lifestyle was an example to us of how to seek his kingdom first. Everywhere he went, his home country of heaven followed, on earth as it is in heaven, through prayer. "Our citizenship is in heaven" (Philippians 3:20), and we have been given the same rights as Jesus to bring heaven to earth through our prayers.

Jesus began his ministry and encouraged his disciples to preach "The kingdom of heaven is at hand. Heal the sick, cleanse the lepers, raise the dead, cast out demons. Freely you have received, freely give" (Matthew 10:7–8). "Most assuredly, I say to you, he who believes in Me, the works that

I do he will do also; and greater works than these he will do, because I go to My Father"
(John 14:12).

We've all been invited to pick up where Jesus's ministry left off and bring heaven to people who are in great need of love, hope, healing, freedom, and restoration. How do we seek the kingdom (God's reality)? By inviting heaven to come crashing through someone's hardships or circumstances in life. Jesus said the kingdom of God is within you (Luke 17:21). God has put eternity in the hearts of all men (Ecclesiastes 3:11). Seek the kingdom of heaven through quiet times with God. Read his Word and worship, but also seek heaven inside others by praying for them. Jesus prayed for people and heaven (God's reality) showed up. Do you see heaven in other people? Look for it, because heaven is here, waiting for the citizens of heaven to pray for people again, just like Jesus did.

PRAYER

Father, help me to always seek heaven first. Show me how things are done in heaven, what's in heaven that I can access down here, and when you want me to pray for heaven to come to earth for the people around me.

DAY 33

THE BLESSING OF HIS FACE

NUMBERS 6:24–26 NIV

The Lord bless you and keep you; the Lord make his face shine on you and be gracious to you; the Lord turn his face toward you and give you peace.

INSIGHT

When I went through my DTS school (discipleship training school in YWAM—Youth With A Mission), I remember them telling me DTS really stood for "die to self." When you walk with God long enough, he'll ask you to do stuff you don't want to do. God always sees the beginning and the end. He sees your potential and what you're capable of. He knows what you need to do. When you truly embrace the face of God, you're willing to do anything to please him.

The people of the ancient world knew you would die if you looked at the face of God, but they also knew you would be blessed with peace. How could an experience so serious kill you but give you peace at the same time? Perhaps they were given glimpses of the coming Messiah and knew the blessing of forever walking in his glance.

My pastor quoted the verse for today all the time when I was growing up, and I sometimes thought, *Why does the pastor use the same Scripture over and over at the end of the service*? Little did I know he was speaking a blessing over us before we went home. Living in the face of God is the blessing our forefathers and mothers looked forward to. This blessing was everything to them, and God reminds me of this blessing every day.

PRAYER

God, I pray you would bless me and keep me, that you would make your face shine upon me and give me peace. Thank for your blessing over my life and my family's lives for generations to come!

DAY 34

ENCOUNTER THE HEALER

ISAIAH 53:5

But he was pierced for our transgressions, he was crushed for our iniquities; the punishment that brought us peace was on him, and by his wounds we are healed.

INSIGHT

God heals people because of his love for his kids. His heart is always to heal and restore what was lost. God heals because Jesus's sacrifice on the cross made healing on earth possible. "By His wounds we are healed" (Isaiah 53:5).

God loves it when we step out in fearless faith. We're presented with so many opportunities in this life to stand in the gap and pray for God to heal someone. Sometimes it's about finding out what God is saying in that moment and doing exactly what he's told us to do. I've noticed the more I step out to pray for people, the more God shows up.

Everyone's invited to pray for the sick and injured to be healed. Is there going to be that person who doesn't get healed? Sure, but so many people are afraid of God not showing up to heal someone that they don't even try. They're already backing up on their heels and doubting God's ability and goodness. I've always challenged that mindset and have turned it around by saying, but what if God decides to show up instead? Is he going to catch me praying just like him and then back me up with his healing hand?

We make it way too complicated when it comes to healing. There are so many more reasons why God heals somebody vs. why he doesn't, so today I want you to set your expectations really high and begin taking risks outside your comfort zone. Unless God tells you not to, I want you to pray in a very aggressive way for everyone who needs healing. You may need to pray for a few hours at home after laying hands on someone, or you may get God's insight for that person in your dreams the night before. God and his angels are waiting on your prayers so they can heal people. Step out today and watch and see what God does!

PRAYER

God, I pray for your healing presence to heal everyone you want me to pray for. Give me the courage to step out and take risks today, regardless of the outcome. It's by your wounds that we are healed!

DAY 35

THE SPIRIT OF THE LORD IS ON ME

ISAIAH 61:1–3

The Spirit of the Sovereign Lord is on me, because the Lord has anointed me to proclaim good news to the poor. He has sent me to bind up the brokenhearted, to proclaim freedom for the captives and release from darkness for the prisoners, to proclaim the year of the Lord's favor and the day of vengeance of our God, to comfort all who mourn, and provide for those who grieve in Zion— to bestow on them a crown of beauty instead of ashes, the oil of joy instead of mourning, and a garment of praise instead of a spirit of despair.

INSIGHT

If there's a Bible verse I would want to brand me for life, it would be Isaiah 61. When Jesus started his ministry, he stood in front of a synagogue of people and read it out loud. He was almost stoned to death for it, because he was implying he was the long-awaited Messiah. All of us eventually need to stand up and proclaim this verse over our lives, regardless of people wanting to stone us with their words, because we have the same anointing and mission as Jesus.

After you give your life to Jesus and invite the Holy Spirit to dwell inside you, he comes upon you to minister to the multitudes, which is a different experience. The *indwelling* of the Holy Spirit is for you, the Holy Spirit *upon* you is for others. Holy Spirit rested upon many people in the Old Testament, and they were invisible on the battlefield and off, but they accomplished a lot.

The Holy Spirit is the greatest power on earth! The Holy Spirit is fully *God* and lives inside those of us who call ourselves followers of Christ, or Christians. In the beginning, the Holy Spirit was hovering over the waters of the deep and whenever God spoke things into existence, the Holy Spirit created them. In the same way, things are created on earth as they are in heaven because the Holy Spirit is always hovering, ready to do all the things through us Jesus said we'd do. The Holy Spirit dwells inside us to counsel and comfort us, but he also likes to rest upon us to counsel and comfort others.

PRAYER

Holy Spirit, would you come and fill me with your presence 'til I'm overflowing? I ask that you would rest upon me the way you did with Jesus. Show me how to walk in your ministry, Jesus! Holy Spirit, remove anything that holds me back from experiencing you in the fullest way. Come, Holy Spirit; I love you!

DAY 36

BREAKTHROUGH ENCOUNTERS

MATTHEW 5:3–9

"Blessed are the poor in spirit, for theirs is the kingdom of heaven. Blessed are those who mourn, for they shall be comforted. Blessed are the meek, for they shall inherit the earth. Blessed are those who hunger and thirst for righteousness, for they shall be filled. Blessed are the merciful, for they shall obtain mercy. Blessed are the pure in heart, for they shall see God. Blessed are the peacemakers, for they shall be called sons of God."

INSIGHT

The Sermon on the Mount is our anthem in regard to walking this intimate life with God. Some of the greatest breakthroughs I've seen in the past have been when I've read this paragraph out loud like I believed it. I don't know how to fully explain it, but I've stood toe-to-toe with spiritual giants and won because of declaring this paragraph out loud.

There's a heavenly and earthly alignment that takes place when we're living from the sermon on the mount mindset—one of knowing how blessed we are because we choose to believe his promises. Sometimes God waits for physical obedience before he releases a spiritual breakthrough or encounters. Find out what God is asking of you in this season and do it.

Many times before I pray for people for healing, I'll sense some kind of faith roadblock that needs to be removed before their blessing can come. God's heart, his will, is always to save, heal, and deliver his kids from harmful things. We'll often say oh, I guess it wasn't God's will to heal you. Yeah right. God is more interested in seeing people healed than anybody! He's waiting for you to step up to the plate with the faith he gave you and go for it. God is always bringing heaven to earth to save, heal, and deliver. It's part of his nature.

A lot of times I'll ask the Lord for a word of knowledge (supernatural revelation from God about people's past or present life) to encourage them before I pray for God to heal him. When people see that God cares about the very little details of their lives, their faith skyrockets, and they're suddenly primed with a little strong faith for God to heal them or others.

"And from the days of John the Baptist until now the kingdom of heaven suffers violence, and the violent take it by force" (Matthew 11:12). Sometimes God requires us to get aggressive and push through a roadblock the enemy set up. We need to have faith that God will bring heaven to that person's circumstances and hardships. Sometimes we have to get spiritually violent in our prayer life if we're ever going to see breakthrough encounters!

PRAYER

God, I pray for your breakthrough encounters whenever I face roadblocks in life. I pray for your presence to break through in my circumstances. I pray to see your face, Lord.

DAY 37

ENCOUNTER THE GOD WHO SAVES, HEALS, AND DELIVERS

LUKE 23:42–43

> *Then he said to Jesus, "Lord, remember me when You come into Your kingdom." And Jesus said to him, "Assuredly, I say to you, today you will be with Me in Paradise."*

INSIGHT

Sozo, the Greek word for salvation, has a greater meaning than most of us understand. There are so many verses in the Bible where *sozo* is used to mean salvation, healing, and deliverance. Many people will give their lives to God, but they'll struggle with strongholds like addictions and other things in their lives. Yes, once people give themselves to God and they're under the blood of Jesus, they're saved and their spirit communes with the Holy Spirit; but what I've noticed is when they don't do housecleaning, the enemy can still mess with their soul (mind, will, and emotions).

We must allow God to completely *sozo* us. It's all about surrendering when it comes to doing housecleaning, and about coming out of agreement with lies. All throughout the Gospels, Jesus healed so many people and delivered a ton of people. People don't want to talk about these teachings today because it displeases the world, but I'm not interested in pleasing the world. I'm only interested in pleasing God! Make up your mind who you want to please, man or *God.*

Jesus is the same yesterday, today, and forever. What he said two thousand years ago is still relevant today. If Jesus was here, he would do the same thing in terms of bringing the kingdom of heaven to earth everywhere he went, and people would get saved, healed, and delivered. his mission and his ministry haven't changed. His game plan is the same for today.

If you simply said, Lord, remember me when you come into your kingdom, and meant it in your heart, you'd better believe the author of life would be moved with compassion for you. God looks at the condition of your heart and sees everything. If you want to be free from addictions, then cry out to God for his presence, his power, and his grace to battle for you. If you want to be free from bondage, then repent, change the way you think, and command every unwanted guest in your spiritual life to leave in Jesus's powerful name. Guys, this is not pretending, this is kingdom reality. The manifest presence of Jesus knocks the devil straight out of your life, and then everything changes from the inside out.

"Today salvation has come to this house, because he also is a son of Abraham; for the Son of Man has come to seek and save that which was lost" (Luke 19:9–10).

PRAYER

Find some prayer warriors you trust, and set aside some time and just go for it. Lay hands on one another and pray for the manifest presence of God to show up. He (the Holy Spirit, God) will help you navigate through the appropriate prayers in your time together. Be bold and be excited, for God is about to do something awesome in you!

DAY 38

GOD WILL ENCOUNTER THE WORLD THROUGH YOU

1 JOHN 4:8

God is love.

INSIGHT

An old friend of mine from Bethel Church in Redding, California, once said to me, "If you want to move in kingdom power, you need to first learn to move in kingdom love." Deep down inside us all lies a desire and longing for love that outweighs everything this world has to offer. When pursuing a relationship with God and people, our motive must be love. Whether we're coming near God to hear what he's saying to us or to others around us, love trumps everything on earth and heaven, because love is a person.

Everyone on earth is waiting for an encounter from God. There's a never-ending appetite for the miraculous growing across the globe. Young and old people are getting bolder in their prayer lives and expecting impossible things to happen in the name of Jesus. As people begin to step out in radical obedience, radical miracles begin to happen daily. All of a sudden, this is now considered normal Christianity. The challenge will be whether we do it with love or not. God invites all humanity into his family and calls us his kids. If you've been wondering what God looks like, go take a look at all humanity. God doesn't wish that any should perish but that all would come to the saving knowledge of Jesus Christ (2 Peter 3:9).

I'll often feel God's love for someone before I pray for the kingdom to show up, which I'm grateful for. "Though I speak with the tongues of men and of angels, but have not love, I have become sounding brass or a clanging cymbal. And though I have the gift of prophecy, and understand all mysteries and all knowledge, and though I have all faith, so that I could remove mountains, but have not love, I am nothing. And though I bestow all my goods to feed the poor, and though I give my body to be burned, but have not love, it profits me nothing" (I Corinthians 13:1–3).

PRAYER

God, I pray you would help me love like you. Give me your heart for all humanity. Let me show the world your beautiful face, God.

DAY 39

WALKING IN ENCOUNTERS

ACTS 1:8 NIV

"But you will receive power when the Holy Spirit comes on you; and you will be my witnesses in Jerusalem, and in all Judea and Samaria, and to the ends of the earth."

INSIGHT

Normal Christianity looks like the book of Acts and beyond. I think Jesus picked Peter, probably an average fisherman who swore like sailor, to lead the church, because he saw a man who had the potential to be like an immovable rock. Did Peter get scared when his life was at risk, when he was walking on water, when he was denying Jesus? Yes. But the difference between Peter and the rest of the disciples was he never hesitated to take risks. I'm pretty sure it's safe to say Peter was a risk-taker and wasn't afraid of much.

Jesus is looking for risk-takers like Peter, because he knows they'll go for it. If you want to walk in daily encounters with God, you have to take risks way beyond your comfort zone. The Holy Spirit will equip you with everything Jesus walked in, yes—*everything* Jesus walked in. "Very truly I tell you, whoever believes in me will do the works I have been doing, and they will do even greater things than these, because I am going to the Father" (John 14:12 NIV).

A lot of people go out there with the idea that their slick and persuasive words somehow are going to have a bigger impact on someone than if they surrender to the promptings of the Holy Spirit. Paul put it like this: "My speech and my preaching were not with persuasive words of human wisdom, but in demonstration of the Spirit and of power, that your faith should not be in the wisdom of men but in the power of God" (1 Corinthians 2:3–5).

"I light myself on fire and people come watch me burn" (John Wesley). Walking in encounters requires risk after risk. The risk you'll face and overcome each time is a part of process God allows to develop your faith history. So each time you're faced with something, the Holy Spirit will remind you of what you overcame last time. Develop your faith history by taking risks every day, based on the promptings the Lord shares with you.

PRAYER

God, I pray for the faith of Jesus to go after everything you have for me in life. I pray your perfect love would cast out fear and you would help me take risks every day of my life. Give me the courage to walk in the ministry of Jesus Christ. God, show me your face as I step out in great faith to pray for people.

DAY 40

FACE TO FACE

NUMBERS 12:6–8

Then He said, "Hear now My words: If there is a prophet among you, I, the LORD, make Myself known to him in a vision; I speak to him in a dream. Not so with My servant Moses; He is faithful in all My house. I speak with him face-to-face, even plainly, and not in dark sayings; and he sees the form of the Lord."

INSIGHT

God spoke clear as day to Moses, as a friend speaks to his friends. As I said in an earlier chapter, in the Old Testament, no could see the face of God and live. But "the Lord spoke to Moses face-to-face, as a man speaks to his friend" (Exodus 33;11). Today I want you realize that God offers you the same type of relationship, only better! We have *all* been given the ability to hear and see God. We were made in his image so that we may share his heart with all humanity. We've all been invited to sit down with God and talk with him as a man speaks with friends.

Today, would you surrender to everything God has for you in life? I know it may feel hard to do, but he's absolutely in love with you. Everything about you fascinates him. He's not mad at you, he only wants to be with you. You were made specifically to live right next to him. The main event of your life is the unveiled smile of Jesus looking at you; it's about being transformed into who he truly created you to be. Maybe you saw his face of love as a child, through a friend, or through defending the weak. Take another look, because he's never taken his eyes off you. God's been looking at you your entire life!

When one of the disciples asked Jesus to see the Father, Jesus replied, "Don't you know me?" Jesus allows us to look into God the Father's eyes again, just like Adam and Eve did in the garden.

Those who decide to chase after God will be ruined for anything they experienced originally in life. When we behold God, part of us dies and we become like Jesus. "Those who look to him are radiant" (Psalm 34:5).

Today, behold and become like Jesus. You were created to live in his presence and to walk in a lifestyle of constantly encountering the face of *God.*

PRAYER

God, I want to surrender everything I am and everything I have to you. Thank you for your love. Thank you that I can see that love face-to-face every day from now on. Thank you that I get to be like Jesus.

ABOUT THE AUTHOR

Richie Root is the founder of Kingdom Mindset. His passion is to inspire and train a generation of people to take on this journey of intimacy with God and see heaven invade earth. He has spoken to audiences internationally about the Holy Spirit, the kingdom of heaven, social justice, hearing God's voice, and equipping believers in the purposes of God. Richie and his wife have two girls and live in Cincinnati, Ohio.

CONTACT RICHIE

WEBSITE: richieroot.com
FACEBOOK: facebook.com/richierootministries
E-MAIL: richieroot@gmail.com